KUNDAI Z. CHIKOWERO

SHINE YOUR LIGHT

Poems of hope, encouragement, peace, and determination.

To dad, mom, Anesu, and Takunda.

For all my family and friends, and for the teen in me.

Hangs in the Air

Martin Luther King Jr had a dream
A dream he would still have, had he
been alive
But since he is not here to transform
it
It just hangs in the air!

It hangs in the air waiting
Waiting for someone to grab onto it
Make it a vision
Then a reality
As of now, the dream hangs in the air!

A reality that will transform America
America will transform into a nation of
equality
With fairness and justice for all
Old, young, poor or, rich
In this country it will not matter
All that will matter is what's on the
inside

But for now the dream hangs in the air

Until then we have work to do
Work to do, to enlighten one another
Until everyone is treated the same
The dream hangs in the air!

Until we learn to embrace one another
Embrace one another, with genuine
respect
Black, white, men or, women
Together we can rise up as a nation
Sadly, for now the dream hangs in the
air

Martin Luther King Jr. had a dream
A dream he would want fulfilled, and
come to fruition
Until we see beyond skin color,
religion, or nationality
The dream hangs in the air!

September 2, 1945

We Surrender

We want peace

One by one

We end the fight

No more bullets, bombs, or guns
Just candy, games and let us play ball
Let us have a party and make some
noise
Parade the streets with glee and joy

For WW2 shall be no more
Open windows and let the fresh breeze
in

Get rid of all our dirty rags

Let us raise the flags

All the countries are at peace

Germany will not be left aloof
Every September 2nd, let us sit down
and recollect

Memories of our ancestors

Let us learn from their mistakes
Peace, happiness, and joy, let us

spread, instead
We dance
We celebrate
One by one
We strive for peace

I Am Hephaestus

I am Hephaestus, son of Zeus
Who was flung onto the Island of
Lemons by Zeus
I am Hephaestus, gentle and skilled
Who is very fond of his mother
I am Hephaestus, big and strong
Who built two mechanical robots with
kids of their own
I am Hephaestus, husband of
Aphrodite
For whom I sit and fashion clothes
I am Hephaestus, a brave god
Who stepped between my arguing
parents
I am Hephaestus, hard working and
peace loving
Who is the god of smiths and fire

Be the Light!

Shine your light, and take control
You might be a girl, let nothing stop
you
Shine that light, and keep it shining
Learn science, technology, math and
engineering
Shine your light, and hold the reins
Learn to code, learn to program
Shine your light, and be a leader
Learn to fly, let nothing stop you
Shine that light, and never tire
Learn and inspire other girls world
over
Shine your light, and take control
You might be a girl, still shine that
light

Realization

I spent some time wondering
Why my dream wouldn't come
I spent precious hours thinking
When will someone do that?
Used good time asking
Why can't I be like them?
I lost amazing moments
Watching someone else succeed
Lost beautiful days
With my head down to the ground

Now I spend time chasing
My wildest, biggest dreams
I'm using my time to realize
That I am somebody
I'm using amazing hours
Being the only ME there is
I'm making precious memories
Watching myself succeed

Enjoying beautiful days
With my head opposite the ground

Move on Forward

Tumble, flip, stick, salute
Upside down or on the ground
You're full of anticipation
Levels one to elite
Training long and hard
Until your adventures feel complete

If you choose to keep on forward
That's amazing!
Good for you
Forty hours a week
School as well
Sometimes overwhelming
But in the end
It's worth the effort

Here you are

It's now or never

Defeat your obstacles

Move on forward

From head to toe

Covered in chalk
How hard do you want to know?

Who will be on top

Bring home the gold
And comes success for you

Moments of Reality

Everyday
Every month
I think of what I truly want

I see it in my dreams
Imagine it a night
Wondering just when
Will I get to take my flight?

Can it become reality
Or is it really unrealistic
If I reach to grab it
Will it just disappear?

Every morning
Every week
Every night
And every month
Waiting for reality
Will I get there?

Reality Check

Not too long ago
I was a child
Untouched by the world and its greed
Bugs were actually fascinating
Dreaming sweet dreams
Unaware of a full life ahead

Now I'm a teen
Still quite sweet
But everything is changing
Terrifying things
Thrown straight at me
Left, right, and center

Bugs can bite you
Enemies stare you down
Too far in the ocean?
You may drown
Everyone is judging you

But you know what?

Who cares

Nobody decides what I am

Only I have that choice

Only I have the power to do so

So if you have a problem
Then I guess that's too bad for you

Now soon I'll be an adult

Will I be invincible?

No

But I'll be pretty close
This world has some good in it too
Even if you have to dig to find it

Open Minds

You'll be happy when you set yourself
free

Open minds are key
Because these days everyone is a judge
Everyone is a critic

Whether you listen

Is your own choice
You are your own person

And you have a voice
But whether or not you use it
Is your decision

It's Okay

It is okay to be different
Different is unique
Different is amazing
But it isn't a flaw

"No one is perfect"
Guess what?
That is a lie
Everyone is perfect
Just for those and the beloved around
them

Open your eyes
And look around
Nobody's the same
Even if they act like it
Everyone is amazing
In their own special way
Look in the mirror
Because everyone includes you

Iceberg

I am an iceberg
Small at the top
Greatest features hidden

I am something onlookers will not
notice
Only known by those
Who will stop to know a person

I may look small
But really, I am enormous
Filled with ideas
It's one of those things
That everyday people won't ever know

First

Make me your number one
Make me useful
It'll be the best thing
You have ever done

Pay attention
And don't forget to mention
How much you'd regret
If you ever let me go

Because I'm a balloon
Full of ideas
And open to more
But you let me go
And I will be gone
Only to fall back
In a completely different place

So hold on tight
And never let me go
Because I will go where the wind takes
me

And most of the time
Wind will not go in circles

Wide Closed

I am a closed book
My knowledge hidden within
Ignored by most
But I have ideas
Ideas that will fill your glass
Up to the brim

I am like grass
And I can catch fire
Constantly stepped on
Constantly cut
But no matter who walks over me
I can and will grow back
Stronger and fresher than before

I am also like glass
You can easily shatter me
Into millions of pieces
So shatter me to shards
I will fight back

I may break
Or I may snap
But I come back stronger
Like acid rain
Even broken

Equal Meaning the Same

How come people are treated unfairly
with disrespect and inequality
If only everyone was treated with
equality,
this would be a better universe

Words such as racist and prejudice
would not exist
There would be no hate crimes against
one another
And when there would be a problem,
People would solve it.
Peacefully.
Safely.
Just like Martin Luther King Jr.
wanted

He had a dream
A dream in which he wanted to fulfill
Although he could not,
that does not make it impossible for
us

For you, me, and everybody else
It doesn't take a whole lot
Just a little from everybody
How do we know when his dream is reality?
When there is equality and justice
When we see everyone as equal
"Equal'' meaning the same

Sophisticated

Mighty, Powerful
Vivacious, Brave
Daring, Raring

A girl who is eager,
Eager to try new things
Eager to explore
Ready to conquer
The mighty wondrous seas

Dazing, Dizzying
Eye-opening, Inspiring

A girl who is eager
Eager to learn new things
Eager to open her mind
Ready to discover
The mighty world of knowledge

Mighty, Powerful
Raring to conquer new heights

Ode to Awesomeness

Born a genius, born to shine!
Smart, bold, creative and awesome
Born to discover and be innovative

Young, bold, brainy, smart

The universe is the limit
Never stop!

Ode to Light

Dark, then Light
Hate, then Love
War, then Peace
Illuminate and conquer darkness

Wash away all the ignorance
Bring in peace
With light, all darkness is gone
With love, all hate is gone
With peace, all the wars are gone

Light, peace, love!

Let it shine

Let there be light in our countries
Let there be light in our nations
Let there be light in our continents
Let there be light in our universe
Let there be light the world over

I see light

I hear peace

I smell kindness

I feel love
Imagine a world filled with darkness!
Let there be light in our hearts!

Ode to the Ocean

Peaceful, calm, blue, and never ending
Imagine, such peace!
Calming fulfilling
Peaceful and quiet
Imagine, such peace!
The breeze, the sound
The depth the length
Miles of calmness, miles of peace
We need a world with such breeze

Laughter

They say it heals,
They say it's the best medicine
Laugh, love, live and thrive
Spread the laughter, share the joy

Laugh, love, live and strive
You may be going through raging
storm
Laugh, learn, explore and thrive

They say we need it
They say it heals
Laugh, explore, learn and explore.

Love

Love who you are
You are unique
Embrace who you are
For there is only one you

Like an eagle, fly high with courage
Courage to love, love who you are
Like an aeroplane, fly high above
Fly high above with a heart filled with love

Hold on to what matters most
You do matter, you are unique
You are who you are
For there is only one you

Love yourself, and embrace who you are
For there is only one you

Sun

It Glows
It Warms
It Heats
Across the nations
Warmth comes in abundance
It warms our nations
It warms our bodies
It warms our hearts
It warms our souls
Now I wonder,
Why is there so much darkness?

At Times

At times
I wonder, why so much hate
1 oh, I wonder, why not so much love!

At Times
I wonder, why so much darkness
oh, I wonder, why not so much light!

At times
I wonder, why so much coldness
oh, I wonder, why not so much
warmth!

At times
I wonder, why wars, wars and more
wars
oh, I wonder, why not peace, and more
peace!

Hope

Looking up
high up in the sky,
it is all blue, bright and endless
I see hope.

Looking up
high up in the sky,
I see all blue, a cloudless sky.

Looking up
high up in sky,
I shed a few tears,
They are tears of hope.

Hope
for the future
for love
for peace
for a bright future
for all generations.

I believe, there is hope.

Hope for a better tomorrow, hope for our planet, and hope for our universe!